First Facts

EASY MAGIC TRICKS

INCREDIBLE TRICKS AT THE DINNER TABLE

by Steve Charney

CAPSTONE PRESS
a capstone imprint

First Facts is published by Capstone Press,
151 Good Counsel Drive, P.O. Box 669, Mankato, Minnesota 56002.
www.capstonepub.com

Books published by Capstone Press are manufactured with paper
containing at least 10 percent post-consumer waste.

Library of Congress Cataloging-in-Publication Data
Charney, Steve.
 Incredible tricks at the dinner table / by Steve Charney.
   p. cm.—(First facts : easy magic tricks)
 Includes bibliographical references and index.
 Summary: "Step-by-step instructions and photos describe how to perform magic tricks
with items from a dinner table"—Provided by publisher.
 ISBN 978-1-4296-4516-4 (library binding)
 1. Magic tricks—Juvenile literature. 2. Tableware—Juvenile literature. I. Title. II. Series.
 GV1548.C44 2011
 793.8—dc22   2010003664

Editorial Credits

Kathryn Clay, editor; Matt Bruning, designer; Marcy Morin, scheduler;
  Sarah Schuette, photo stylist; Eric Manske, production specialist

Photo Credits

All photos by Capstone Press/Karon Dubke, except Ed Hord, 24

Printed in the United States of America in North Mankato, Minnesota.
022011   006089R

TABLE OF CONTENTS

INTRODUCTION

What's on the menu tonight? Magic! Magic at the dinner table can save the day. There's no need to be bored waiting for the food to come. Just look around the table for a few **props**.

Here's a tip for you, not for the waiter. Don't be boring. Leave that to the meatloaf. Think of a good story. Make up jokes. Then practice, practice, practice.

Listen for the dinner bell. If it's time to eat, it's time to perform magic.

prop—an item used by a performer during a show
magician—a person who performs magic tricks

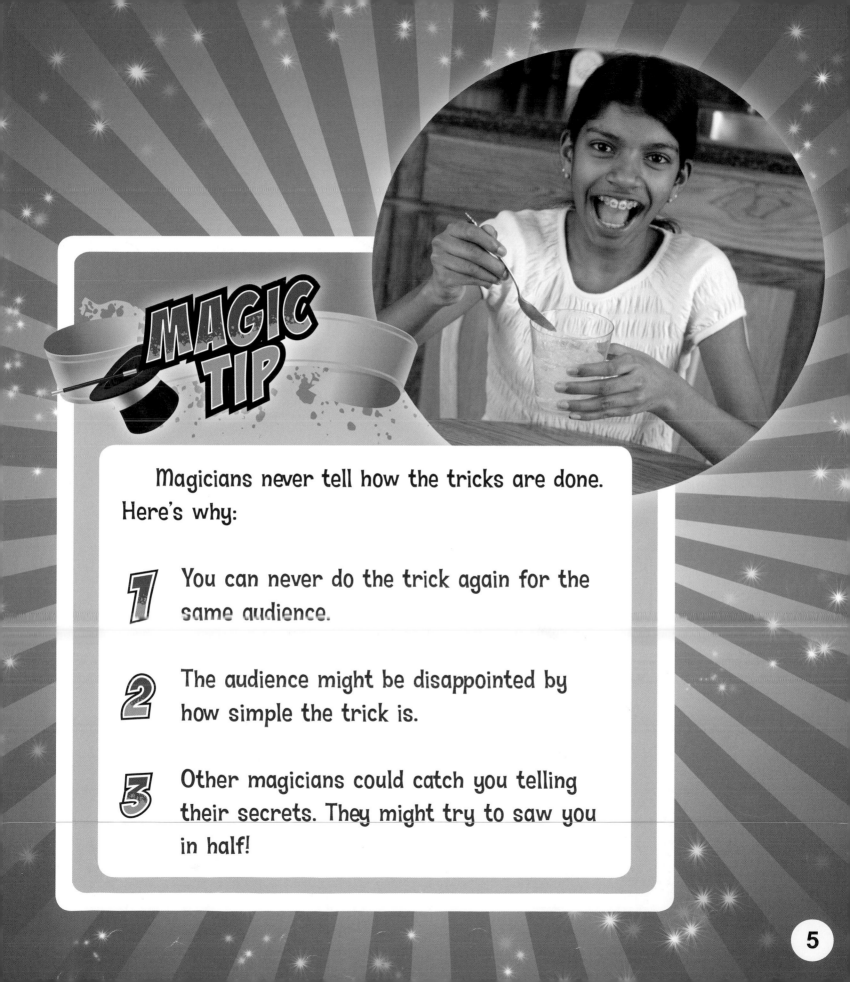

MAGIC TIP

Magicians never tell how the tricks are done. Here's why:

1 You can never do the trick again for the same audience.

2 The audience might be disappointed by how simple the trick is.

3 Other magicians could catch you telling their secrets. They might try to saw you in half!

THE SHAKER TAKER

When someone asks for the salt, make the saltshaker disappear. Just use a coin for **misdirection**. Your dad will be looking at the coin, not the saltshaker.

Materials: a coin, a saltshaker, a paper napkin

The Trick:

1 Place a coin on the table. Put a saltshaker on top of the coin. Say, "I can use a saltshaker to make a coin go through the table."

2 Cover the saltshaker with a napkin. Hold the napkin and bang the top of the shaker with your other hand.

misdirection—to draw attention to a spot where the trick is not taking place

3

Lift the napkin and shaker near the edge of the table. The coin is still there. Say, "I'll try again."

4

Put the napkin and shaker on the coin again. Bang the top of the shaker.

5

Hold the napkin and shaker over your lap. Loosen your grip. The shaker drops into your lap. The napkin keeps the shape of the saltshaker.

6

Say, "This coin is tricky. I'll try once more." Place the napkin over the coin.

7

Smash the top of the napkin. The coin is still there, but the saltshaker disappeared!

BALANCING ACT

Have you **balanced** on one foot before? With a little magic, this cup balances on the edge of a plate.

Materials: a dinner plate and a plastic cup

The Trick:

1

Hold a plate in front of you with your left hand. Wrap four fingers around the front of the plate. Your thumb is behind the plate.

balance—to keep steady and not fall

Hold the cup on the edge of the plate with your right hand.

Secretly move your left thumb to the bottom of the cup. Your thumb helps hold the cup in place. Take your right hand off the cup.

The plate hides your thumb, so the cup looks like it is balanced on the plate.

MAGIC TIP

Use a plastic cup. A glass cup could break if it slipped.

THE LAST STRAW

How do you make a straw move without touching it? Just use your mind.

Materials: a drinking straw

The Trick:

1

Place a straw on the table. Say, "I can move this straw with my mind." Trace a circle around the straw with your finger three times. Move your face closer to the straw as you make the circles.

2 Place your fingers behind the straw.

3 Slowly move your fingers away from the straw. As you do this, secretly blow on the straw. Don't let anyone see you blowing.

The straw will roll in the direction of your finger. The straw looks like it moves on its own!

MAGIC TIP

Don't blow too hard or make noise. People will figure out the trick if they see you blowing.

A REALLY COOL TRICK

A glass of water instantly turns to ice. How cool is that?

Materials: plastic wrap, a glass of water, a book, and a spoon

Getting Ready:

Crumple up a piece of plastic wrap. **Palm** it in your left hand.

The Trick:

1

Set a glass of water on the table.

2

Place an open book in front of the glass. Your friend should no longer be able to see the glass.

palm—to hide something in your hand

3 Secretly drop the plastic wrap into the water. Tell your friend that stirring the water will turn it into ice.

4 Stir the water with a spoon. Stirring will unfold the plastic wrap.

5 Say, "Freeze!" Remove the book. The plastic wrap will look like ice in the water.

MAGIC TIP

Having trouble hiding the plastic wrap in your hand? Try wearing a long-sleeved shirt. You can hide the plastic wrap in your sleeve.

STICKY FINGERS

How do you make a spoon float? It's easy.
You just need sticky fingers.

Materials: a spoon

The Trick:

1 Hold a spoon in your left hand. The back of your hand faces the audience.

2 Say, "To do this trick, I'll need a steady hand." Grab your left wrist with your right hand. Secretly place your index finger over the spoon handle.

3 Say, "My hand is sticky like glue. It will keep the spoon from falling." Slowly open up your fist. The spoon doesn't fall.

4 Move your hand up and down. The spoon looks like it's moving.

5 Close your fist and remove your left hand. Ta-da!

MAGIC TIP

A thin breadstick or a pencil will also work.

THE GREAT GRAPE

How do you balance a fat grape on a skinny finger? It's easy. Just use a magic grape.

Materials: a toothpick and a grape

Getting Ready:

Point your index finger up. Secretly hide a toothpick behind your finger. Use your thumb to hold the toothpick in place.

The Trick:

Say, "I will balance this magic grape on my finger." Pretend to balance the grape as you push the toothpick into the grape.

2

Move your hand as if it's difficult to balance the grape. Keep your palm facing you to hide the toothpick.

3

Remove the grape, and let your friend try. When she's not looking, hide the toothpick in your pocket.

MAGIC TIP

Don't have any grapes nearby? Try this trick with any food that can easily be pushed onto a toothpick.

NEW-AGAIN NAPKIN

Anyone can rip up a napkin. But only a magician can put the pieces back together.

Materials:
two paper napkins and a spoon

Getting Ready:

Crumple one napkin into a ball. Put a spoon in your back pocket.

The Trick:

1 Palm the crumpled napkin in your left hand. Don't let anyone see the napkin.

2 Tear the second napkin in half.

MAGIC TIP

Having trouble hiding the napkin in your hand? Try hiding the napkin in your back pocket. You can grab it when you reach for the spoon.

3

Tear the napkin in half again.

4

Crumple the pieces into a ball with your left fist. Now you have two napkins in your left hand.

5

Say, "I will put the napkin back together!" Grab the whole napkin with your right hand. The whole napkin will be on the bottom of your left fist.

6

Say, "Oops, I forgot my magic wand." Reach behind you with your left hand. Put the torn napkin in your back pocket. Then grab the spoon.

7

Wave the spoon over your right hand. Open your hand to show the napkin. It's whole again!

CLINK DRINK

Don't believe everything you hear! This coin only sounds like it was dropped in a glass.

Materials: a coin, a cloth napkin, and a drinking glass

The Trick:

1

Show your friend the coin. Then cover the coin with a cloth napkin.

2

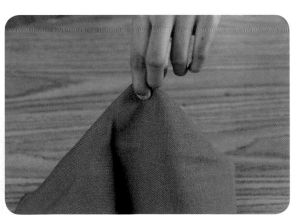

Pick up the napkin while pinching the coin underneath.

3 Place the napkin and coin over a glass. Say, "I will drop the coin into the glass. Listen."

4 Secretly **tilt** the glass in your hand. Drop the coin so it hits the side of the glass with a "clink." The coin will drop into your hand, not the glass. Your friends will think it dropped into the glass.

5 Put the covered glass on the table. Remove your hand with the coin palmed in it.

6 Say, "Abracapocus!" Lift the napkin. The glass is empty and the coin disappeared!

tilt—to lean at an angle

GLOSSARY

audience (AW-dee-uhns)—people who watch or listen to a play, movie, or show

balance (BA-luhnts)—to keep steady and not fall

magician (ma-JI-shuhn)—a person who performs magic tricks

misdirection (mis-di-REK-shuhn)—to draw attention to a spot where the trick is not taking place

palm (PALM)—to hide something in your hand

prop (PROP)—an item used by a performer during a show

tilt (TILT)—to lean at an angle

READ MORE

Becker, Helaine. *Magic up Your Sleeve: Amazing Illusions, Tricks, and Science Facts You'll Never Believe*. Berkeley, Calif: Owlkids, 2010.

Charney, Steve. *Hocus-Jokus: How to Do Funny Magic*. Minnetonka, Minn.: Meadowbrook Press, 2003.

Fullman, Joe. *Sleight of Hand*. Magic Handbook. Laguna Hills, Calif.: QEB Pub., 2008.

INTERNET SITES

FactHound offers a safe, fun way to find Internet sites related to this book. All of the sites on FactHound have been researched by our staff.

Here's all you do:

Visit *www.facthound.com*

Type in this code: 9781429645164

INDEX

ABOUT THE AUTHOR

Steve Charney learned magic when he was a little kid. Now he performs more than 100 times each year.

Steve is also a ventriloquist, radio personality, musician, and songwriter. He has written songbooks, storybooks, joke books, and magic books. Look for his performances on the Internet.

Being Considerate

by Jill Lynn Donahue   illustrated by Stacey Previn

PICTURE WINDOW BOOKS
Minneapolis, Minnesota

Special thanks to our advisers for their expertise:

Kay Augustine
National Director and Character Education Specialist, Ignite
West Des Moines, Iowa

D., Professor of English
Minnesota State University, Mankato

Editor: Shelly Lyons
Designer: Tracy Davies
Page Production: Michelle Biedscheid
Art Director: Nathan Gassman
Associate Managing Editor: Christianne Jones
The illustrations in this book were created with acrylics.

Picture Window Books
5115 Excelsior Boulevard
Suite 232
Minneapolis, MN 55416
877-845-8392
www.picturewindowbooks.com

Printed in the United States of America.

 All books published by Picture Window Books
are manufactured with paper containing at least
10 percent post-consumer waste.

Library of Congress Cataloging-in-Publication Data
Donahue, Jill L. (Jill Lynn), 1967-
Being considerate / by Jill Lynn Donahue ; illustrated by
Stacey Previn.
p. cm. – (Way to be!)
Includes bibliographical references and index.
ISBN-13: 978-1-4048-3777-5 (library binding)
ISBN-10: 1-4048-3777-9 (library binding)
1. Thoughtfulness—Juvenile literature. I. Previn, Stacey.
II. Title.
BJ1533.T45D66 2008
179'.9–dc22   2007004588

Being considerate means caring for other people, thinking about their feelings, and trying to help them. Considerate people are respectful and use good manners. There are many ways to be considerate.

Benny's grandma is sick. Benny comes home after school and makes her a card.

Benny is being considerate.

4

Blake sets the table for dinner. He knows his mom has had a long, hard day.

Blake is being considerate.

While the neighbors are away on vacation, Roland waters their flowers.

Roland is being considerate.

Lee drops Evan's ball in the mud. Lee says he is sorry and uses the garden hose to wash away the dirt.

Lee is being considerate.

14

Carlos broke his arm while skateboarding. Joy helps Mom bake cookies to make Carlos feel better.

Joy and Mom are being considerate.

Maria's father worked all night at the hospital. Maria plays quietly so he can sleep.

Maria is being considerate.

16

It rains while Sarah
and Jan wait for
the school bus. Sarah
shares her umbrella
with Jan.

**Sarah is
being considerate.**

19

Madison and her family camp at a state park. They clean up after themselves before they go home.

Madison and her family are being considerate.

At the school carnival, May buys some cotton candy.
May shares her cotton candy with her little brother.

May is being considerate.

To Learn More

At the Library

Brimner, Larry Dane. *The Sidewalk Patrol*. New York: Children's Press, 2002.

Schuette, Sarah L. *Consideration*. Mankato, Minn.: Capstone Press, 2005.

Seskin, Steve, and Allen Shamblin. *A Chance to Shine*. Berkeley, Calif.: Tricycle Press, 2005.

On the Web

FactHound offers a safe, fun way to find Web sites related to this book.
All of the sites on FactHound have been researched by our staff.

1. Visit www.facthound.com
2. Type in this special code: 1404837779
3. Click on the FETCH IT button.

Your trusty FactHound will fetch the best sites for you!

Index

Look for all of the books in the Way to Be! series:

Being a Good Citizen

Being Brave

Being Considerate

Being Cooperative

Being Courageous

Being Fair

Being Honest

Being Respectful

Being Responsible

Being Tolerant

Being Trustworthy

Caring

Manners at School

Manners at the Table

Manners in Public

Manners in the Library

Manners on the Playground

Manners on the Telephone